SURVIVOR

Alive!
Airplane Crash in the Andes Mountains

Scott P. Werther

HIGH
interest
books

Children's Press®
A Division of Scholastic Inc.
New York / Toronto / London / Auckland / Sydney
Mexico City / New Delhi / Hong Kong
Danbury, Connecticut

Book Design: Christopher Logan
Contributing Editor: Eric Fein

Photo Credits: Cover, pp. 8, 16 © Bettmann/Corbis; pp. 4, 23
© Michael Carr/Index Stock Imagery, Inc.; p. 11 © Barnabas
Bosshart/Corbis; pp. 15, 19, 29, 30, 35, 36, 39 © Corbis Sygma;
p. 24 © Galen Rowell/Corbis; p. 40 © Reuters/Max Montecinos/Corbis

Library of Congress Cataloging-in-Publication Data

Werther, Scott P.
    Alive! : airplane crash in the Andes mountains / Scott P.
    Werther.
    p. cm. — (Survivor)
    Includes index.
    ISBN 0-516-24329-2 (lib. bdg.) — ISBN 0-516-27869-X (pbk.)
    1. Survival after airplane accidents, shipwrecks, etc.—Juvenile
    literature. 2. Aircraft accidents—Andes Region—Juvenile
    literature. 3. Cannibalism—Andes Region—Juvenile literature.
    I. Title. II. Series.

    TL553.9 .W47 2003
    982'.6—dc21
                                              2002153229

Contents

Introduction   5

1 Plane Crash in the Andes   9

2 Struggling to Survive   17

3 Disaster Strikes Again   25

4 The Long Walk   31

Timeline   41

New Words   42

For Further Reading   44

Resources   45

Index   47

About the Author   48

The Andes mountain range extends for 5,500 miles
(8,851 kilometers) along the western coast of
South America.

Introduction

The air is so cold that the simple act of breathing hurts. The pain in your broken leg is unbearable. A few days ago, the airplane you were flying in crashed high up in the Andes Mountains on its way to Chile. Now, you and the other survivors huddle together inside the remains of the plane. Almost everyone is injured. All are cold and scared. Some of the survivors are dying.

Days pass. There is no sign that help is on the way. What little food there once was is gone. The only way to survive is to find your own way off the mountain. With every passing hour, you and the other survivors grow weaker. Some survivors think the situation is hopeless—that you will all die up here in the mountains. Another group would hear none of that. Where there is life, there is hope, they say. They are determined to find a way out of the mountains. They will do whatever is necessary to survive—even eating the dead passengers' flesh to keep up their strength. The thought of doing this is horrifying, but there is no alternative—except death.

The days turn into weeks. You and the other survivors continue to battle the fierce cold. Each brave attempt at leaving the mountains ends in failure. All of the careful planning to escape your icy prison is for nothing. You watch as the number of your fellow survivors becomes fewer with each passing day. You wonder if your turn to be counted among the dead will come. You count the passing days as if they were a death sentence.

Your chances of survival are almost zero—and you know it. Yet you also know that you *must* not give up the hope that you will soon be rescued. You desperately cling to that hope. Without it, you will surely die.

Flight Through the Andes
October 12–October 13, 1972

1 Plane leaves Montevideo, Uruguay, for Santiago, Chile
2 Due to bad weather, plane lands in Mendoza, Argentina
3 Plane crashes high in Andes Mountains

Santiago

Mendoza

URUGUAY

ARGENTINA

Montevideo

CHILE

CRASH SITE

Area of Detail

Many of the passengers on the ill-fated plane were from Montevideo. Montevideo is the capital of Uruguay.

One

Plane Crash in the Andes

On October 12, 1972, a plane left Montevideo, Uruguay, flying west for Santiago, Chile. The plane was a Fairchild F-227, a twin-engined turboprop. The plane carried forty passengers and five crewmembers. Sixteen of the passengers were members of a college rugby team from Uruguay. Traveling with them were friends and family. The team was on its way to play a rugby match in Chile. Due to reports of bad weather, the plane landed in Mendoza, Argentina. The passengers spent the night at local hotels in Mendoza. The next day, the weather cleared. The plane took off at 2:18 P.M. In a little more than an hour, disaster would strike.

To reach Santiago, the plane had to cross the Andes Mountains. The Andes is a beautiful, snowcapped mountain range that rises to great heights. Flying across the Andes would be dangerous because the plane could not fly higher than 22,500 feet (6,858 meters). One of the mountains on the way to Chile was 22,834 feet (6,960 m). To cross the mountains, the plane would have to fly through a pass between mountain peaks. Also, the weather in the mountains could get very dangerous. Strong winds could blow a plane around as if it were a piece of paper.

As the plane approached a ridge of mountains, shifting pockets of warm and cold air caused it to make sudden drops in elevation. In the plane's cabin some of the players were walking around, joking, and tossing a ball. Following the pilots' instructions, the steward asked the passengers to take their seats and put on their seat belts.

Suddenly, a large cloud surrounded the plane. The plane quickly dropped several hundred feet. Passengers looking out of the plane's windows were shocked by what they saw: The wing of the

Santiago, the capital of Chile, is one of the biggest cities in South America. About five million people live there.

plane was only 10 feet (3.04 m) above the mountains! The pilots desperately tried to pull the plane up, but they couldn't. Some of the terrified passengers started to pray. Others braced themselves for the coming crash.

Seconds later, the right wing hit the mountain. It was instantly ripped off. The wing smashed into the tail of the plane and ripped that off as well. Five people fell out of that opening. A moment later, the left wing was ripped off, too. The body of the plane crash-landed on its belly, sliding along a snowy valley like a sled. At the time it hit the ground, the plane was traveling at about 230 miles (370 kilometers) per hour. Two more people fell out of the back of the plane. The force of the crash ripped many of the seats from the floor. These seats crushed and killed some people caught between them.

Remarkably, the plane skidded to a stop just before it could smash into a rock face. Roberto Canessa, one of the rugby players, was the first to recover from the shock of the accident. All around him people were laying unconscious or dead. Some of the other passengers were moaning in pain. Canessa helped his friend Daniel Maspons get out of his crushed seat. Then the two began helping others. Soon, other passengers were also able to help those who were still trapped. Another member of the team, Gustavo Zerbino, was one of the first to help. Zerbino and Canessa were both medical students. It would be up to them to give whatever medical treatment was possible.

A Horrible Sight

When the survivors stumbled out of the plane, they were greeted by a horrifying sight: Snow covered everything as far as they could see. Mountains towered over them on three sides. The situation looked hopeless.

Back in the plane, many passengers were dead or dying. A total of twelve people had died during the crash. A few others were so badly injured that there was nothing that could be done for them. In the coming days, these people would die, too.

The survivors' first night in the mountains would be like most of the nights to follow—freezing. Many of the young men were not prepared for the cold. They were wearing short-sleeved shirts. Cold air blew through the plane's wreckage where the survivors had set up a sleeping area. To keep out the cold, they built a wall of suitcases and snow at the open end of the plane. This would be an activity they repeated every night. Some of the men took the seat covers to make small blankets for themselves. The survivors huddled together to keep warm as they slept.

The same question was on each person's mind: Would the group survive their terrible tragedy?

Did You Know?

The survivors of the Fairchild F-227 plane crash were young. Most were in their early twenties.

The plane's tail section was ripped away from the plane during the crash. In the days that followed, the tail would play an important role in the lives of the survivors.

The survivors turned the plane's wreckage into their shelter. They huddled together to keep warm.

TWO

Struggling to Survive

The survivors knew that rescuers could take a long time to find them. They searched the luggage and the wreckage of the plane for food. They found three bottles of wine and a few bottles of liquor to drink. There were also eight chocolate bars and five nougat bars. The search also turned up caramels, dates, two cans of mussels, salted almonds, and a few jars of jam. These few items were all the survivors had to eat. Marcelo Pérez was the captain of the rugby team. He took the leadership role of the survivors upon himself. He made sure everyone had a fair share of the food.

The survivors turned the plane wreckage into their shelter. They removed seats to make space for people to lie down at night. Crude bowls were made from the metal parts of the seats. Snow was piled into these bowls and left outside to melt in the sun. The melted snow would be used for drinking water.

On October 15, three planes flew over the crash site within a few hours of each other. Each time one passed, the survivors tried to catch the pilots' attention. They screamed, waved their arms, and jumped up and down. At first, they believed that they had been spotted and that help was on the way. As night fell, however, there were no signs of rescue.

Helping Themselves

The survivors soon realized that their lives were in their own hands. They had to find their own way off the mountain. They found maps in the plane. The maps led them to believe that the way out of the mountain was over a nearby mountain ridge. They also thought the tail section of the plane was in that same direction. The survivors believed that a battery that could make the cockpit radio work was in the tail section. If they could get the cockpit radio to work, they

The plane's wreckage was used by the survivors as their base camp.

may be able to call for help. Also, they hoped to find other survivors in the tail section.

On the morning of October 17, four survivors set out to find the tail section. The four were Fito Strauch, Roberto Canessa, Carlitos Páez, and Numa Turcatti. Strauch had a clever plan to use the plane's seat cushions as snowshoes. However, walking on the cushions was difficult and took a lot of energy. The young men were very weak. It had been five days since they had eaten a good meal. They agreed to return to the plane and come up with a better plan. On the way back, the idea of using the dead for food was brought up. As upsetting as the thought was to some of them, it didn't seem like such a crazy idea.

Tough Decisions

October 22 was the survivors' tenth day on the mountain. Starvation had become their greatest concern. Their food was almost gone. Canessa and Strauch announced that they would be willing to eat the dead to survive. The survivors needed food—of any kind—to get the strength to escape the mountains. The flesh of the dead would give them that strength. Many of the others were instantly opposed. Canessa stood firm. He realized that eating the dead was his only chance of survival.

The necessity of the group's difficult decision was made clear the next day. A small transistor radio had recently been found in the plane. The radio had been damaged, but one of the rugby players, Roy Harley, managed to get it to work. The survivors were able to pick up a broadcast of a news report. The report said the formal search for the survivors had been called off. The survivors now had almost no hope of rescue. Many of them cried when they heard the news. Other survivors, refused to panic. It was decided that another expedition to get out of the mountains should be organized at once.

Just over an hour later, Zerbino, Turcatti, and Maspons set off to find the missing tail section. They also hoped to find a way out of the Andes. They spent the night under a rock outcrop. Temperatures were so cold they could not sleep.

The young men feared they would freeze to death. They hit each other to keep their blood flowing.

The next day, the three young men did not find the tail section. Instead, they found one of the plane's engines and the bathroom. They also found the bodies of people who had fallen out of the plane when it crashed. They counted up the number of dead at both this site and the plane. A total of eighteen people had lost their lives. The three also discovered that many mountains still lay to the east and to the north of them. They had hoped they reached the edge of the Andes, but it didn't look that way. Exhausted, they struggled back downhill to the plane. Once again, an attempt to find a way out of the icy mountains had failed.

Wherever the survivors went, there was no sign of life—just snow-covered mountains all around them.

Three

Disaster Strikes Again

In the days that followed, the survivors continued to endure their icy prison. Yet just when
they thought their situation couldn't get any
worse, it did. On October 29, while most of them
were napping, an avalanche hit the plane—
burying it almost entirely. Roy Harley was
instantly buried up to his waist in snow. A few
hands were sticking out from the snow and wav-
ing around. Harley dug out the snow around
Carlitos Páez, who had been sleeping next to him.

Páez was breathing, but he couldn't move
under the weight of the snow. Harley moved on
and dug out Canessa and Strauch. Frantically,
they shoveled out snow around areas where they
thought their friends had been sleeping. Some of
the victims were already dead by the time they
were dug out. For those trapped under it, the

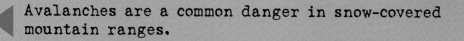

Avalanches are a common danger in snow-covered
mountain ranges.

weight of the snow made moving impossible. Breathing holes were dug for some survivors until they could be totally freed. Unfortunately, some had been buried too deeply. Eight people died underneath the snow. Now, the death toll was at twenty-six.

Hiking to Nowhere

A second avalanche hit the plane an hour later. This one completely buried the wreckage in snow. The survivors were forced to remain within the cramped, bitterly cold plane. Six of the young men managed to dig a tunnel through the cockpit window only to discover that there was a blizzard raging outside. They would have to stay inside the plane until it passed. While trapped under the snow, they ate the flesh of some of those who had died in the first avalanche. The blizzard finally ended on November 1. Clearing the snow out of the plane took eight days.

After the blizzard, the men made preparations for an expedition to hike over the mountain. They spent over two weeks preparing for the trip. Only the strongest would go. On November 17, Canessa, Fernando Parrado, and Antonio Vizintín set off to find help. Their plan was to hike to the west. They believed that was the direction of the closest village. This guess was based on things the pilots had said about the crash area before they died. The mountain to the west, however, was too high for them to climb. They figured the valley below curved back around to the west. They chose to hike down and follow the valley.

It didn't take the trio long to come upon the tail section. That discovery alone made the expedition worthwhile. They found clothing, medicine, chocolate, sugar, and rum. There were comic books and wooden crates to burn for warmth. There were also batteries. The batteries could be hooked up to the radio in the cockpit. Unfortunately, the batteries were too heavy to carry back to the plane.

The men spent the night at the tail section and then continued on. Soon they realized that they had guessed wrong about the valley. It did not seem to curve back to the west. They were hiking farther into the Andes. They turned around and went back to the group at the plane. The survivors decided to remove the cockpit radio and take it to the tail section. They spent several days attempting to use the radio to make contact with the outside world. Once again, however, their hopes were crushed: The batteries they had found in the tail section did not work with the cockpit's radio.

The survivors turned the tail section into their second base as they tried to find a way out of the Andes.

The survivors made many of the tools and
supplies from things that had been retrieved
from the wreckage. The survivor leaning
against the plane is sewing a sleeping bag.

Four

The Long Walk

Another attempt to hike out of the Andes was planned. Canessa, Parrado, and Vizintín would once again make up the expedition. The survivors made a sleeping bag out of some insulating material they found in the tail section of the plane. They packed flesh cut from the dead for food. Also, they took lipstick to protect their chapped lips, maps from the plane, and a medical kit. Each wore a few pairs of pants and as many as six sweaters plus a jacket.

On December 11, another survivor died. This was the third person to die since the avalanches buried the plane. Of the original forty-five passengers and crew members, only sixteen were still alive.

On December 12, Canessa, Parrado, and Vizintín spent two nights huddled together in the homemade sleeping bag. They slept on an uneven mountain slope. On the third day, after climbing a wall of snow that was almost vertical, they reached the top of the mountain. The men were hoping to see green valleys on the other side of the mountain. Yet all they could see were more snowcapped mountains. Despite the awful discovery, Parrado and Canessa were convinced they should push on. Far in the distance were two mountains that did not have any snow on them. The three men reasoned that Chile was somewhere in that direction. Since Vizintín was the weakest of the three, it was decided that he would return to the others back at the plane.

The other side of the mountain was very steep. The walk down was dangerous. At one point, Parrado slid out of control. He slammed into a wall of snow. From then on, both young men slowed down their pace. They huddled together in their sleeping bag as soon as the sun went down. They sipped brandy to stay warm. Canessa was becoming increasingly weaker. He had to stop frequently to rest as they trekked through the mountains.

Out of the Snow

After a few difficult nights, they reached a stream that had grass and moss growing around it. It was the first vegetation they had seen in sixty-five days. Canessa ate a few mouthfuls of it. Soon they reached the end of the valley. There, they discovered a rushing river surrounded by patches of grass and flowers.

For the first time since the crash, they had a strong belief that they would be saved. They pushed on to get help for their trapped friends. On the eighth day of their expedition, they saw a group of cows in the distance.

Canessa felt very sick the next day. Parrado had to help him walk. As the sun set, they built a fire. They discussed killing a cow for meat. Suddenly, on the other side of the river, a strange shape appeared. Parrado ran toward what they believed was a man on a horse. At the same time, Canessa screamed and shouted as loud as he could. Then they realized that there were three men on horseback. Desperately, over the noise from the raging river, the survivors tried to communicate that they needed help. However, the men were herding their cows. Both Canessa and Parrado were very frustrated because they couldn't get the riders to respond to them. Finally, one of the riders said something. The only thing that Canessa and Parrado heard was the word *tomorrow*. The three men left without realizing that they were the survivors' last hope for rescue.

The next day, December 21, the cowherders returned. They brought Parrado and Canessa to their hut down the river. The cowherders fed the two survivors enough food for several grown men. After Parrado and Canessa had eaten, they took a nap. It had been seventy days since their plane crashed in the Andes.

By the time they awoke, one of the cowherders had left. He had gone by horseback to the nearest police station to let authorities know that there

The survivors owe their lives to the cowherders who found them. ▶

were survivors trapped in the mountains. It was determined that a helicopter would be needed to get the other survivors out of the mountains. The next morning, three helicopters arrived. Parrado was afraid to ride in a helicopter. Nevertheless, he agreed to show the pilot the location of the wreck. It was decided that only two helicopters would go on the rescue mission. The third would be used as a reserve, if needed.

¡71 días sepultados bajo la nieve!

¡Resucitamos!

Dijeron llorando Canessa y Parrado en los momentos de volver a la vida

"NOS SALVARON LA FE EN DIOS Y LAS ANSIAS DE VIVIR"

CLARÍN

The rescue of the survivors made front page news on newspapers all over the world.

Rescued!

Flying the helicopters in the mountains was difficult. Heavy winds blew dangerously around them. Finally, the rescuers reached the wreckage. Down below, the survivors ran around shouting to get their attention. The helicopters

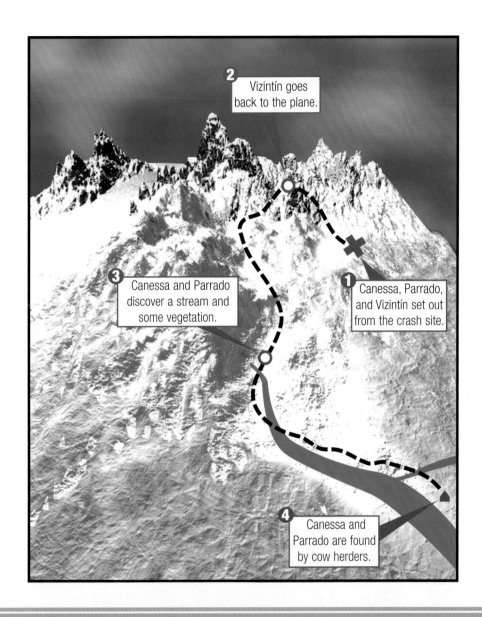

2 Vizintín goes back to the plane.

3 Canessa and Parrado discover a stream and some vegetation.

1 Canessa, Parrado, and Vizintín set out from the crash site.

4 Canessa and Parrado are found by cow herders.

The dashed line indicates the path that Canessa and Parrado took in hopes of finding help. Their journey was about ten days long.

hovered close above the ground. Rescuers jumped out. Six survivors climbed aboard the two helicopters. Eight survivors and a few of the rescuers had to stay at the wreckage because there was not enough room on the helicopters. The next morning, helicopters returned for the final eight survivors.

Soon after the sixteen survivors were airlifted off of the mountain, they were taken to a hospital in San Fernando, Chile. They were fed and treated for their injuries. They were all suffering from malnutrition. However, none of them were

Did You Know?

Many of the survivors have gone on to achieve great success in their lives. Roberto Canessa is one of the finest doctors in Uruguay. Fernando Parrado is a successful businessman and television producer.

in critical condition. Most of their families were waiting for them at the hospital. Journalists from all around the world were waiting to talk to them. Within days of their rescue, the truth came out about what they had eaten to stay alive. Some people were shocked and horrified. Others were more understanding of the survivors' actions.

The survivors were overjoyed to be back home with their families.

The young men had done what was necessary to survive. During their adventure, they experienced enough pain and emotional agony to fill a hundred lifetimes. However, they held on to the hope that they would survive. They did survive because they worked together and cared for one another. They succeeded and lived to tell their tale of survival in the Andes Mountains.

Thirty years after the plane crash, some of the survivors returned to the area to pay their respects. The survivors, from left to right, are: Alfredo Delgado, Jose Luis Inciarte, Carlos Páez, and Roberto Canessa.

TIMELINE

A plane carrying forty-five people crashed in the Andes Mountains. For the next seventy days, the survivors struggled to stay alive. During this time, many died. The rest were forced to eat the flesh of the dead to stay alive. Several attempts to hike out of the Andes ended in failure. Finally, two survivors managed to find a way out of the mountains and get help. Twenty-nine people died in the tragedy.

- **October 12, 1972** The plane leaves Montevideo, Uruguay. It is on its way to Chile. Reports of bad weather force the pilots to land in Mendoza, Argentina.
- **October 13** The plane continues on to Chile. About an hour after takeoff, the plane crashes high in the Andes Mountains.
- **October 17** A small group of the survivors make their first attempt to hike out of the mountains.
- **October 29** Two avalanches bury the survivors inside the plane.
- **December 11** Three survivors set off to find help. After a few days, one of them returns to the plane.
- **December 20** The two continuing survivors see cowherders at work. The cowherders promise to return the next day to help.
- **December 21** The cowherders bring the survivors to their hut.
- **December 22** One of the survivors guides two rescue helicopters to the crash site.
- **December 23** The helicopters return to pick up the last of the survivors.

NEW WORDS

airlifted (**air**-lift-id) to have been transported by aircraft

Andes Mountains (**an**-deez **moun**-tuhnz) a mountain system of South America

avalanche (**av**-uh-lanch) a large mass of snow, ice, or earth that suddenly moves down the side of a mountain

elevation (el-uh-**vay**-shuhn) a high place or a hill

expedition (ek-spuh-**dish**-uhn) a long journey for a special purpose

malnutrition (mal-noo-**trish**-uhn) a harmful condition caused by not having enough food or by eating the wrong kinds of food

nougat (**noo**-guht) a candy made of sugar or honey and nuts

outcrop (**out**-krop) a part of a rock formation that appears out of the ground

pass (**pass**) a narrow passage in a mountain range

ridge (**rij**) a long narrow chain of mountains or hills

starvation (**starv**-ay-shuhn) the state of suffering from lack of food

unconscious (uhn-**kon**-shuhss) not able to see, feel, or think

vertical (**vur**-tuh-kuhl) upright, or straight up and down

wreckage (**rek**-ij) the broken parts or pieces lying around at the site of a crash or an explosion

FOR FURTHER READING

Cobb, Vicki. *This Place is High: The Andes Mountains of South America*. New York: Walker and Company, 1993.

Read, Piers Paul. *Alive*. New York: Avon Books, 1974.

Storm, Rory. *Mountain Survivor's Guide*. New York: Scholastic, Inc., 2001.

Web Sites

Alive: The Andes Survivors

http://members.aol.com/PorkinsR6/alive.html

This site offers a summary of the survivors' story and background material. It also includes photos and information about the survivors' whereabouts today.

¡VIVEN! Accident in the Andes

www.viven.com.uy/571/eng/default.asp

This site offers information on the survivors. There are photos of the group before, during, and after the crash.

Cultures of the Andes

www.andes.org

Find out about the native people of the Andes Mountains and their culture on this Web site. There are also plenty of links to other Andes-related sites.

INDEX

A

Andes Mountains, 5, 9,
 40
avalanche, 25–26, 31

B

batteries, 27–28
blizzard, 26

C

Chile, 5, 9–10, 32, 38
cockpit radio, 18, 28
cowherders, 34
crash, 12–13, 33

D

drinking water, 17

E

elevation, 10
expedition, 21, 26–27,
 31, 33

H

helicopter, 35–36, 38
hike, 26–27, 31

J

journalists, 39

M

malnutrition, 38
maps, 18, 31
medical kit, 31

N

news report, 21

O

outcrop, 21

P

pass, 10
pilot, 10, 12, 18, 27, 35
plane, 5, 9–10, 12–14,
 17–18, 20–22, 25–28,
 31–32, 34

INDEX

R
radio, 18, 21–22, 28
rescue, 21, 34, 39
ridge, 10, 18
rugby team, 9, 17

S
starvation, 20

U
Uruguay, 9

V
valley, 12, 27, 32–33
vegetation, 33

W
weather, 9–10
wreckage, 14, 17, 26,
   36, 38

ABOUT THE AUTHOR

Scott P. Werther is an editor and freelance writer from Monkton, Maryland. He recommends that all readers spend some time in the outdoors.